HOW TO FIND

LOST TREASURE

CHARLES GARRETT

HOW TO FIND LOST TREASURE

© Charles L. Garrett 2006

Third printing: May 2007
First printing: December 2006

CONTENTS

Charles and Eleanor Garrett founded Garrett Electronics in 1964.

ABOUT THE AUTHOR

Treasure hunters listen when Charles Garrett speaks. For more than 40 years he has pioneered the development of the modern metal detector, demonstrated its capabilities in searches throughout the world and devoted himself to teaching others to use detectors. He has discovered treasure with metal detectors of his own design on every continent except Antarctica, and he has also scanned under lakes, seas and oceans of the world. Many of the treasures and relics he has discovered are displayed in the Garrett Museum at the company's factory in Garland, Texas.

Charles Garrett did not set out to become the world's leading manufacturer of metal detection equipment. His lifetime interest in treasure hunting, however, prepared him to excel in that field. After earning an electrical engineering degree, he became busily engaged at Texas Instruments and Teledyne Geotech in developing systems and equipment required by

America's fledgling space effort. While also devoting himself to his hobby, however, he designed and built metal detectors. This avocation became a career when he and his wife, Eleanor, founded Garrett Electronics in 1964 to manufacture and market his inventions.

Garrett quality is known today throughout the world. From the beginning, Charles Garrett vowed "to practice what I preach"— in other words to test his equipment in the field—to insure it will work for customers regardless of ground conditions and environment. He has become recognized as an unofficial spokesman for the hobby of treasure hunting and the metal detecting industry through a long list of honors, personal appearances and books. He is the author of several major works on searching for treasure which have been accepted as veritable "texts." No one is more qualified to give tips to treasure hunters than Charles Garrett.

INTRODUCTION

Finding treasure with a metal detector is simple and easy. The purpose of this little booklet is to help you learn how. You and family members can find treasure if you...

1. Use a quality metal detector, and

2. Make the necessary effort.

Today's metal detectors are almost unbelievably easy to use. Touch a single control pad on a modern computerized instrument and begin finding treasure immediately. You may never have to touch another control. It's that easy to hunt with today's One-Touch instruments!

Yes, that's all there is to it! Moreover, visual target indicators on some detectors report on every target over which your searchcoil sweeps. That's right, you see on your detector screen every target you encounter, and you get an audible alert on those worth digging. Imaging by Garrett® even discloses a target's size!

Now, I'm talking about quality instruments... not the inexpensive "toys" that have discouraged so many people because they just wouldn't find much of anything. And that's what will be discussed in this booklet...quality metal detectors that are, in truth, scientific instruments. Let me just say that I've been using my own high quality detectors to find all sorts of things for more than 40 years, and I'm still amazed at the ease with which our newer models can be operated. Automatic One Touch detectors are so simple that it's sometimes uncanny.

Modern computerized circuitry will find more treasure and will find it quicker and easier than even the best of yesterday's instruments. For more than 40 years, Garrett has designed and manufactured equipment in the continuing progress of metal detection worldwide.

Year by year, breathtaking advancements have been made by the Garrett engineering lab.

The extremely popular Garrett Ace 150 and Ace 250 Metal Detectors offer superior search capabilities at affordable prices.

You see, metal detectors have entered the computer age, and treasure hunting has never been simpler than with a computerized One-Touch detector.

So, for you to succeed as a treasure hunter, first must come the quality detector. If you're using a Garrett instrument, there can be no

The Garrett GTI 2500 Graphic Target Imaging Metal Detector sets the highest standards in treasure hunting.

question about quality. I am confident that my detectors are the best. That's not to say that some other manufacturers don't make quality detectors. They do. But, I don't believe that any of their instruments will match up to a Garrett detector in the same price range. At the same time, unfortunately, there are other detectors on the market (at generally lower prices) that simply can't offer the quality necessary for you to maximize your treasure hunting abilities.

Second, and equally important, is your *desire* to find treasure. You must enjoy being out in the fresh air searching over all kinds of terrain. You must understand and tolerate the aches and pains that come with stooping and squatting as you use a detector to find treasure. You must expect to get your hands dirty when you dig up those treasures. Finally, you must enjoy hunting with a detector out in the field even when you're *not* finding treasure.

You can take my word for it: success will come when you follow these three basic steps:

- **Locate treasure "hot spots" with your metal detector**
- **Pinpoint and correctly identify all buried treasures**
- **Recover each treasure quickly and professionally**

Charles Garrett

Garland, Texas

LOCATE ALL
TREASURE "HOT SPOTS"

How do successful hobbyists know where to hunt? How do they locate all those treasures... rings, coins, pieces of jewelry and other valuable objects?

They look for them where people have been—which, of course, is practically everywhere. Once a person has begun the fascinating hobby of treasure hunting, he or she will no longer need convincing that small and large treasures are waiting to be found. The fledgling treasure hunter will soon have the problem that all experienced hobbyists face, simply too many places to search. When you begin discovering treasure, you will quickly observe that the number of places to search is truly endless.

What are you trying to locate? Is it an earring that your sister or daughter lost last night at a patio party? That will be easy! Or is it an outlaw's cache that was buried many years ago? Now, that target may require some intense research! But, what if you just want to locate lost coins, jewelry or other treasures no matter where they can be found?

Start at Home

Let me emphasize that you should never overlook the possibilities for locating treasure around your own home. Don't make the mis-

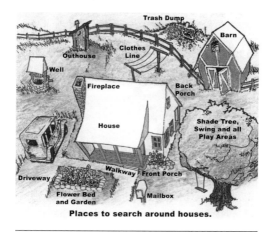

Places to search around houses.

take of believing there are no coins or other treasures to be found where you live. If you don't have the experience now, you soon will gain enough knowledge to convince yourself that treasure is truly located everywhere. The first place every hobbyist should start searching is his own backyard.

Study your local history; talk to the old-timers; determine where old parks, meeting grounds, towns and communities were located. Where did people once congregate? Here, you will locate your personal treasure "hot spots." Here, you will determine where the old and valuable treasure is located...the "stuff" that dreams are made of...that makes treasure hunting really pay off.

About "Hot Spots"

You'll soon discover that treasure "hot spots" can be located in just about any given area. In other words, people have congregated in some places more than others. It's true today; it's always been so. You can learn about "hot spots"

People lose coins and jewelry at playgrounds. Search these areas on a regular basis. There is treasure waiting to be found!

simply by observing people as they go about their daily routines. Drive over to your school or college campus. When you are at church, watch the people coming and going...see where they stand and talk, where their children run and play, where cars let out passengers. Just a little common sense and observation will enable you to increase your finds.

In a children's park or playground, some of the better places to search are under swings, slides and gymnastic equipment. Naturally children who turn head over heels are going to lose coins and jewelry. Such items are also commonly lost in picnic areas where people sit or lie down.

Your imagination will be called on when you investigate areas that are no longer used by the public. From your own experiences, try to visualize where the crowds would have gathered. Then develop "crisscross" metal detection techniques that will let you sample the particular areas you have selected. As you search different areas, keep accurate count of the coins, jewelry and other treasures you find and where

Old abandoned buildings or homesteads are excellent locations to find lost coins and other treasures. Always get permission before searching on private land.

you found them. From this data you will soon learn the probable location of the best places to search. Successful hobbyists seem to be able just to walk into an old park and immediately begin scanning their detector over the exact spot where treasures are to be found. This is a product of experience, and experience will enable you to become such a treasure hunter!

Where were the old schools or meeting places located 50 or 100 years ago? At what locations did people gather in the past where they no longer meet today? What about old military training areas, CCC camps, reunion grounds, settlers' encampments—once lively communities that are now ghost towns? And, what about the ghost towns of yesterday that have totally disappeared today? The growing urbanization of America has caused many thriving rural communities to cease to exist completely...literally to vanish from the face of the earth. Crops in the field grow silently where busy people once congregated, transacted business and lost treasure!

In your home town, where are the long-forgotten fairgrounds, circus and carnival locations...the tent shows that were so popular in the days before air conditioning? What about the old swimming pools and picnic areas? Where were the old train, interurban and bus depots where so many commuters regularly removed coins and tokens from their pockets? There is no way that any single individual can learn of all the rewarding treasure hunting areas in a community. What about nearby parks? How old are they? Are they in the same place now they were 50, 75 or 100 years ago? Check the official records of your city. Investigate vacant lots. What used to be there? As you drive through rural communities and small towns, stop to talk with the old-time residents. And listen to them!

Use Your Ears

Make it a habit to listen to the old-timers. Talk to family, friends, storekeepers—especially the older, retired people of the community who were postmen, bus drivers, merchants, policemen, firemen and the like. These individuals will have a wealth of information that can help you locate valuable treasure hunting areas. And don't ask them simply where you can find old treasure. If they could answer that question, they'd go find it themselves! Just try to start the old-timers talking about the past...their activities and pleasures of yesterday. You'll be amazed at how many are just waiting for an audience. Let them tell you where the general stores, saloons, banks and cafes used to be. Allow them to tell

Charles Garrett searches along a trail in Utah used by stage-coaches and outlaws such as Butch Cassidy and the Sundance Kid in the 1800s.

you of all the things that people used to do. That old-timer won't know it, but he'll be telling you where lost treasure is located, just waiting for your metal detector.

Remember, if you think that you know where a family heirloom is concealed or a treasure might be buried, don't talk about it. Don't even mention it. Keep those stories to yourself and find the items sometime later.

Personal Examples

Let me give you an idea of what I mean. My wife Eleanor grew up in the the little East Texas community of Pennington. About one-half mile from this town is the site of long-gone Steele Academy, a training school for boys that operated for many years before its doors closed long ago. This has proved to be a good treasure hunting area for me.

From a museum curator in the historic town of Cripple Creek, CO, I found the location of an old picnic ground, high above the city on a mountain top. This park and picnic area was once so popular that the local trolley car company built a track all the way to the park and had cars running continuously, especially on weekends. Think how many treasures, 75 and 100 years old, that lie there awaiting the avid treasure hunter.

In my own area of Dallas, I am familiar with parks that have been in use since before the turn of the century. Here I have recovered numerous valuable treasures. Surely you know of similar parks in your areas.

One excellent method for finding the oldest treasure is to locate geographically where your town or city was located when it was founded. Often the present center of the town's activity is far removed from the original center of population. For example, the original town of San Diego, CA, is a few miles north of the present downtown area.

When my family and I visited "Old Town" San Diego and talked with a local Garrett dealer, he showed us where he had excavated at the site of old buildings to uncover many artifacts and valuable treasures.

A friend and his wife in Florida determined the location of the original site of Tampa. Many relics and treasures, including Spanish reales, half dimes, large cents and coins of other denominations were found there. The American coins are dated in the 1830s. Even older coins could still be found because the original town of Tampa was erected just outside Fort Brooke's walls in 1823.

The Older the Treasure, the Better

There is no doubt that most treasure hunters truly enjoy getting out into the parks, playgrounds and other outdoor areas simply to search for lost coins, jewelry and other valuables. And, they delight at every discovery! But, let's face it, the finds that we enjoy most are those with the greatest value. This lets us benefit financially from the hobby. Thus, it behooves us to make the most diligent efforts to locate the treasure hunting areas where the greatest number of targets with the most value are to be found. Granted, each of us experiences a thrill when we dig up a single coin, even if it is of current vintage and worth only face value.

I hope that each of you share my special joy in finding something old...a remnant of the past. The half cents, large cents, two and three-cent pieces, half dimes, Liberty-seated quarters...and especially gold coins. These are often worth many times, often thousands of times, their face value...yet they provide an additional historical and romantic thrill. Such treasures are seldom located in parks, around school yards or in areas of relatively recent occupancy. You must look for the earliest habitations and areas of activity to find these older and rarer treasures. This is where research pays off!

Your Research

Make it a daily habit to read the lost and found sections of newspapers, no matter where you find yourself. Quite often persons losing valuables will advertise and post a reward for the return of their property. You can contact them and make prior agreements concerning

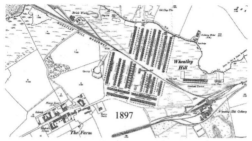

Old maps can reveal the location of places where people once gathered and where they probably lost valuables.

your remuneration or reward if you can locate their lost valuables. Newspapers, too, are filled with information of the locations of public congregations (company picnics, family reunions and other such gatherings).

Spend time at the local library or newspaper office reviewing the issues of yesteryear. You will learn the location of old parks and playgrounds, band concert sites, fairground and circus lots, along with information on public activities that occurred in the past. Notices of lost articles are also to be found here. Only your enthusiasm will limit your efforts and your success. And, if you are a dedicated treasure hunter, you will discover many heart-fluttering stories that suggest veritable bonanzas. May you find some of them!

It's a good idea to make contact with local police and insurance agents or even insurers and law enforcement officials who are not in your immediate area. Tell them you have a metal detector and that you are willing to help them locate lost jewelry and other valuables. You may be surprised at the services you can perform, as well as the rewards you will receive. This is just another example of how the owner of a metal detector can increase his annual income with only a reasonable amount of thought and physical effort.

It may be, too, that insurance agents will tell you the location of a ring or other valuable items that were reported lost and not found.

It's Up to You

There is no way that I can stress strongly enough the importance of the ideas presented in this guide. Sure, treasures are just waiting to be

---

found nearly everywhere, and I am certain that each of you will find a goodly number of them. Still the maximum monetary value in treasure hunting, and the greatest personal rewards, come from finding the old, valuable treasures... and finding them as a result of your own research, investigation and hard work.

True, you'll probably never actually grow tired of discovering coins and treasures of any age...no matter how many of them you find in parks and play grounds. But, you'll get so much more pleasure and larger rewards from recovering old and rare treasures in places you have located through your own desire and careful investigative efforts. You can only grow even more enthusiastic as your rewards increase!

One important technique I learned personally and from talking with successful treasure hunters is to be patient. If at first you aren't finding much treasure, don't fret; be persistent. Keep on searching and try to continually improve your skills. I assure you that your efforts will be rewarded. By the time you have hunted for treasure for 100 hours, your abilities to find

Searching beaches and lake shores can result in profitable discoveries. Wherever there were people, there's a good chance you will find lost items.

treasure will produce results that will amaze and astound you. Keep at it!

Park superintendents and other caretakers can be a valuable aid in treasure hunting. In addition, they will come to love you because you are helping keep their park clean. Often when these individuals learn what you are doing and realize you are actually helping them remove surface trash from the park, they will give you valuable information you can use to find treasure more successfully. They may be able to tell you where people have congregated and, consequently, where lost coins and jewelry are most likely to be found. They can tell you the former location of picnic tables, playground equipment and other centers of activity that might help you locate those valuable treasure "hot spots."

Always carry a pen or pencil and paper to make notes of your finds and ideas that come to mind as you hunt with a metal detector.

From the beginning of your metal detecting career, get into the habit of "logging in" your finds. You should keep track of not only the good stuff you find but also the junk. As you become more experienced with your detector, you will be able to observe the growth of your success. When this begins to happen, you'll notice the ratio of "good" to "bad" finds increasing on the "good" side. The better you understand your detector's signal, the more junk you will be able to leave in the ground. Thus, a daily record is valuable to show your progress and allow you to keep score as you watch accumulations of coins and other valuables grow day by day.

In metal detecting, like anything else, you learn by doing. As you hunt, you will discover your mistakes and you will develop your own particular style with new and better ways to find and recover treasure.

Finally, a couple of important points on treasure hunting locations:

1. NEVER TRESPASS. Every square foot of land in the United States is owned by some individual, group, firm or governmental body. In addition to understanding regulations that govern local, state and federal land, always get permission before hunting on any private property. This is particularly true of any property controlled by the military or other governmental bodies. Remember, you can't pay close attention to your detector's signals if you're listening for a siren!

2. FILL ANY HOLE that you dig. Even more importantly, I urge every treasure hunter to leave any area where you hunt in better condition that you found it.

I have tried to stir your imagination about the great potential of treasure hunting...to help you understand how coins, jewelry and other treasures can be found everywhere. I hope that you will understand, however, that some effort is required if you are to receive any benefits from treasure hunting. Much effort will be necessary to achieve the maximum benefits. Research, planning and a great deal of investigative work and thought will be required. Hit or miss random searching won't be productive. I can't repeat enough the simple truism that your success depends entirely upon your effort. The treasures are there; it's up to you to locate them!

Next, we'll learn how to...

PINPOINT AND IDENTIFY BURIED TARGETS

Using a metal detector to search a site to find the treasures that you think you have located requires persistence and use of proper hunting methods. I can't stress enough the importance of developing these special techniques that fit you and your instrument.

You must learn all about your detector and practice with it to achieve the best results. Read the owner's manual for your instrument not once but several times. Watch the video that came with your Garrett detector and then study it. Follow this by using your detector. In our Garrett owner's manuals we recommend that you build your own test plot. Bury several items including a nail, a piece of foil, a pulltab, a bottlecap and several coins at depths of about one to four inches and a foot apart. Use some sort of indicator to clearly mark the location where each article is buried and even draw a map. Practice scanning the targets while listening to and studying all of your detector's detection signals.

How Detectors "Report"

When you scan your searchcoil over the ground or in the water, a detector reports information on targets in various ways:

• Increases in audible volume (universal on all detectors);

• Graphic information presented visibly; or

• Meter deflections (types of meters can vary greatly, along with the amount and accuracy of the information they present).

Good targets will generally be announced by a clear and distinct tone while the detector will produce "blip-like" or other sounds for pulltabs and similar small trash.

Getting Started

With a One-Touch Garrett detector you're ready at once to hunt for treasure. And that's what you should do!

---

1. With the searchcoil held a foot or two above the ground, just touch one control—the power touchpad—and you're ready to hunt. Lower your searchcoil and begin scanning.

2. Keep the searchcoil level as you scan and always scan slowly and methodically; scan the searchcoil from side to side and in a straight line in front of you with the searchcoil about one-half to one inch above the ground. Do not scan the searchcoil in an arc unless the arc width is narrow (about two feet) or unless you are scanning extremely slowly. This preferred straight-line scan method allows you to cover more ground width in each sweep and permits you to keep the searchcoil level, especially at the end of each sweep. This method reduces skipping and helps you overlap the areas you have scanned more uniformly.

3. Overlap by advancing the searchcoil as much as 50% of the coil's diameter at the end of each sweep path. Occasionally scan an area from a different direction. Do not raise the searchcoil above normal scanning level at the end of each sweep. When the searchcoil begins

Scan side to side with the coil about 1 inch above the ground and walk ½ to 1 foot per second.

to reach the extremes of each sweep, you will find yourself rotating your upper body to stretch out for an even wider sweep. This gives the double benefit of scanning a wider sweep and gaining additional exercise.

4. As you scan the searchcoil over the ground, move the coil at a rate of about one foot per second. Don't get in a hurry, and don't try to cover an acre in 10 minutes. Always remember that what you are looking for is buried just below the sweep you are now making with your searchcoil. It's not some place across the field.

Swinging a Coil

Most detector operators—beginners, I'm certain—swing their searchcoil in front of them in an arc, with the coil often rising at the end of each sweep. More experienced hobbyists move their coil in front of them in a straight line. I prefer the straight line method because I consider it far superior to swinging a coil in a arc. When you scan using a straight-line sweep, a much wider path can be covered in a single scan; the coil can be held at a more uniform height throughout the full scan; and the hobbyist can cover an area more efficiently without skipping spots.

Of course, select your own scanning technique; but if you haven't tried scanning a straight line with your searchcoil, see for yourself how much better it is. You may find it awkward at first, but you'll soon get the "swing" of it!

Cover the Area

If you are confronted with a large area, and you are not sure if that area will be productive for coins or other treasures, it is best to crisscross it with a few well-planned passes. One method is to make a complete pass across one side of the area. Then move over about ten feet and make a second pass parallel to the first. Make notes, and maybe mark with a golf tee, where you find treasure...exact location, depth, etc. Never begin scanning in any large area until you have done all you can to determine where the exciting treasure "hot spots" are.

Garrett's LCD, called a Graphic Target Analyzer, will show you every target—even the "bad" ones for which it makes no sound. The display above shows a quarter at 6+" depth.

Experienced treasure hunters utilize several techniques to make certain they have completely searched a large area. Sometimes they block it off into smaller areas, either mentally or by using some sort of markers. The smaller areas are then searched, one at a time, until the entire large area has been covered. In places where there are trees, benches and other natural markers, use them as your guides. That makes it easier to scan the ground completely without any skipping. In open areas such as large fields and parks, you'll have to furnish your own markers.

Some hobbyists drive small stakes (or golf tees) into the ground and tie strings between the stakes. They make their first pass along the length of the string with the side of the searchcoil touching it. At the end of each strip, move the string over the width of your searchcoil and repeat the process. Some people utilize only the sticks in the ground and leave off the string, which is satisfactory for short distances. The more experienced you become, the easier it will be for you to search large areas. You will rely less and less on such markers as sticks and strings—which you must be sure to discard after you finish scanning. If there are other park visitors, do not use any string, which could cause someone to trip.

Cover the entire area you intend to search. You must! Don't be in a hurry. Remember, the coins you are looking for and hurrying to find on the other side of the park may be right at your feet. Take your time and do a thorough job of searching.

Finding a Target

Meters and LCDs can provide additional information concerning the possible "value" of targets. Garrett's LCD, called a Graphic Target Analyzer (GTA), will show you every target—even the "bad" ones which may not produce a sound if your detector is so adjusted. And the GTA on this precision instrument actually indicates what you've discovered. That's right there's a Target ID Guide located above the LCD. With a GTI detector, you'll even be given an indication of the size of your target. These are just ways in which the GTA and GTI detectors have revolutionized treasure hunting. As detectors continue to improve, I believe that even more target information will be presented visually.

Remember that a quality detector will never "lie" to you. It will simply report what is beneath its searchcoil.

It's up to you to interpret this information. This will be a snap if you're using a detector with a system of visual identification. A glance at its LCD and Target ID Guide should give you a pretty good idea of what you've found...even its size if you're using a GTI.

Depth of Detection

How deep can a metal detector find metal? When an electromagnetic field flows out of the searchcoil several factors determine whether detection is possible: electromagnetic field strength, target size, surface area of the target and the type of metal in the target. How far the electromagnetic field flows from the searchcoil also depends on the size of the searchcoil, quality of its construction and materials that are present in the earth. Larger searchcoils produce a more extensive field that can penetrate more deeply to detect deeper treasures.

Simply stated, the larger a metal target, the better and more deeply it can be detected. It is realistic to expect that a coin-sized target can be detected under normal conditions to depths of six to nine inches. Yet detection is often inches deeper and, sometimes shallower, because of such variables as ground mineraliza-

The 4.5" Super Sniper coil works well in trashy areas because its size covers a small area, helping to eliminate junk targets.

tion, soil moisture and the target metal's conductivity—or even how the target is lying in the ground or how long it has been buried.

Super Sniping

Many treasure hunters have realized they can find even more coins and similar sized treasures with smaller coils. I'm talking about Garrett's famed 4.5-inch Super Sniper™ searchcoil. This small coil can search tight, narrow locations that won't accept larger searchcoils. In addition, it works especially well in trashy areas because the coil's small size lets it cover only a small area that can't include too many junk targets. Remember that a searchcoil reports on all targets in the search matrix that lie beneath it. Remember too, when there are a lot of trash items, good coins can be masked.

When the Super Sniper coil was first made nearly 40 years ago, our engineers envisioned it as a coil to find tiny gold nuggets...which it has! Hobbyists (including me) in search of coins, jewelry and other treasures quickly learned about the new, smaller coil and have since used it to a far greater extent even than we electronic prospectors for whom it was intended. One East Coast hunter found more than 100 coins scattered among hundreds of junk items around the foundations of a destroyed apartment complex. The coil's small size and its powerful, highly concentrated signal were the main factors in making these finds.

Treasure hunters using the Super Sniper have learned to work more slowly and methodically and to expect a little shallower detection depth.

This small treasure-finding wonder makes a welcome addition to any hobbyist's arsenal of metal detecting accessories because it will make discoveries that larger searchcoils may miss or incorrectly identify.

Working Near Metal

Because of its small size, the Super Sniper lets a treasure hunter work closer to such metal items as fences, playground equipment, parking meter and sign posts and buildings with metal siding. When a hobbyist is hunting with an $8^1/2$-inch or larger coil, the metal in these objects may prevent scanning up close, unless that operator knows how to deal with this situation. Here's what I recommend.

Search with your detector as you normally would until it begins to respond to the nearby metal object. When this occurs, adjust your audio volume down into the quiet zone and scan parallel to the object. Listen closely for the increase in sound that will indicate a target. Since few treasure hunters have mastered this technique, or know anything about it, you might find yourself with a real bonanza in some of your regular hunting spots. The Super Sniper searchcoil offers the most effective method for scanning close to metal objects.

Pinpointing and Target Identification

Some detectors offer a mode called automatic pinpointing that aids in locating a target more precisely. Automatic pinpointing enables the instrument to hover directly over a target with only a little motion necessary. Many hobbyists, especially old-timers, prefer to pinpoint their targets manually, even when their detector offers the automatic feature. Pinpoint your target by scanning back and forth over the spot where you got a signal. Draw an imaginary "X" over this spot and dig there. To help you dig a target you should use electronic pinpointing whenever available. Moreover, the target's *identity* will be shown more accurately if you pinpoint it *before* trying to read its identity on the target ID scale.

Now that you've zeroed in on some promising targets, it's time to learn just how to...

RECOVER EACH ITEM PROFESSIONALLY

You've done your research and found your "hot spot." You've used the right metal detector and have received a strong signal. You're positive that you've located a coin or maybe something even more valuable. It's pinpointed; so, what next?

Well, dig, of course. What kind of advice have you heard about digging for treasure? How about these good suggestions:

"Don't use a screwdriver...it'll scratch!"

"Never use a knife...you'll ruin the sod!"

"Always use a probe...less damage to the sod!"

"Don't scratch your treasure with a probe!"

Sounds confusing, doesn't it? Well, let me confuse you just a little more by telling you that all of the above advice can be accurate. It just depends on what you're digging for and the kind of turf into which you're digging! The

Learn which digging tools and techniques work best for you and remember to fill the hole after you dig a target.

problem treasure hunters face when it comes time to dig is that each type of soil requires, generally, a different digging and retrieval technique. Retrieving coins and jewelry from a sandy beach, of course, is fairly easy. Digging items out of hard-packed clay under thick St. Augustine grass may be the most difficult. Retrieval in good, loose dirt under a growth of Bermuda grass lies somewhere between the two extremes.

My treasure-hunting expeditions have taken me from frozen turf in the Far North to sandy Caribbean beaches, and I've stopped at lots of places in between. I understand a great many of the different techniques. They must be learned by any treasure hunter who wants to work with maximum efficiency. I wish I could tell you that somewhere in these journeys I had discovered a magic solution for digging. But there is none. It just represents work...sometimes harder than at other times...but always work. The only consolation is that there is often a fine and immediate reward for digging with the proper tools!

Your Tools

Of course your most important tool will be a high quality modern metal detector. Your sec-

A probe or screwdriver, a trowel, and a coin pouch or apron are all essential tools for the treasure hunter.

ond most important accessory will be the specific implements with which you choose to dig. Among the useful tools that you will ultimately need for locating and recovering treasure are a probe, knife, screwdriver, trowel, weed sickle, apron with at least two pockets, small flashlight, a trash bag or two and—don't laugh—a lawnmower. You will soon learn why you will require different types of digging tools for different types of ground conditions. A sickle or weed cutter is a handy item to have because quite frequently you will encounter bushes and clumps of grass you must remove in order to scan an area properly. If you search at night, you may need a flashlight. The trash bag is good for dumping your trash into when there are no other containers available.

Now, I'm not suggesting by any means that each coin hunter carry around a big power lawn mower. (Maybe you could ride to your hunting location on it!) But, seriously, I would venture to guess that the day will come when you would gladly mow the area where an old abandoned fruit and vegetable stand once existed, or the yard of an old house in order to search these potential hot spots. It is at these types of locations that you will find the older and more valuable treasures.

In addition, you will need a small bag suspended from your belt, or a coin-hunting apron with at least two pockets made either of waterproof plastic or with plastic pocket liners to keep moisture from soiling your clothing. Quite often you will be digging in areas that are wet. When you retrieve treasure from the ground, especially muddy ground, some of the soil will stay with the item until you have an opportunity to clean it. This accumulation of damp soil can cause the contents of non-waterproofed pockets to leak through onto your clothing. I strongly recommend that you protect your clothing (and especially your knees) with comfortable, adjustable waterproof knee pads.

Always carefully determine into which pocket you will be placing valuable finds and into which one you will be placing the trash (bottle caps, nails, pop tops, foil and such that you will occasionally encounter when you retrieve your treasures). Recover and properly dispose of all junk you find because it is likely you will return to the same spot to search again, or another coin hunter will try his luck there.

Over the years I've asked many treasure hunters—men and women whose ideas and opinions I respect—for their thoughts and secrets on digging. I suppose I was quietly hoping that I'd eventually find one who had discovered the magic. Alas, none had. However, they continue to produce such an excellent general discussion of recovering valuable items of treasure as well as presenting a number of interesting techniques for digging in specific types of soils, that I offer all our ideas to you.

You will note in reading about these various techniques that several of the hobbyists use different methods in either probing or retrieving. Keep in mind these individuals have worked out their own recovery methods for speed, ease of recovery, minimum damage to treasure and sod. One method which may work over one given type of sod may not be the best for another type. A method that one person may love could be totally unsatisfactory for somebody else. Study them all; practice them all; and select the method you prefer in the area you work.

Some treasure hunters are lucky enough to live near ocean beaches where tourists come to swim, sun bathe, frolic and lose coins, jewelry and other valuable personal items. Remember that every one loses things—even metal detector hobbyists. Successful beach hunters

Treasure hunting on the beach can be more successful with a wire-mesh scoop-sifter to strain the sand. It recovers both metallic and non-metallic treasures.

have worked out a technique for the recovery of these lost objects. They use two tools, a wire mesh scoop-sifter and a small trowel.

When they have pinpointed the metallic object with their detector they can make one pass through the sand with the sifter if the sand is loose. Zingo! The object is in the sifter, just waiting for the loose sand to be shaken out. Unfortunately, this method doesn't work too well in wet, saturated sands near the water. Here's where the trowel is brought into play.

After pinpointing, they insert the trowel several inches into the ground and with one quick twist "plug" the beach sand, remove the plug and remove the target from it. Rarely does a beach hunter attempt any digging with bare hands in either dry or wet sand. It's quite a temptation, especially in fine, loose sand that looks so warm and inviting. There's just too much broken glass and other sharp objects that will cut into fingers and hands. How about gloves? Most treasure hunters say that they're too hot, especially on the beach. So, it's the sifter and trowel in the sands of ocean beaches.

Here's a recovery tip for lawns and grassy areas: when you locate a metallic object below a grassy surface, cut a half-circle around it and make it three inches deep. Then literally fold the turf back. If your find isn't in this first plug, remove a second and deeper plug, making certain that all loose dirt falls back into the hole. After you retrieve your treasure, fold the turf back in place and step on it.

You'll find that this method is especially good with Bermuda grass which tends to die when you cut a full circle in the grass because it often kills the roots. Of course, you will never put trash back in holes for someone else to dig up. That's why many treasure hunters always wear an apron with two pockets...one for keepers and one for trash.

If you must cut a plug, some hobbyists recommend that you cut it square so that it will fit precisely back into the hole. They suggest further that the plug be cut deeply with lots of soil attached to it so that powerful lawnmowers can't pull your plug from the ground before the grass has become reestablished.

Experience has proven that cone-shaped (pointed at the bottom) plugs are more likely to be uprooted by mowers. Also, you might want to try to pinpoint your find in the plug itself after you dig it up. Then removal can be more exact, and you won't have to break apart the plug to find your target. The more dirt that is left on the plug, the more likely the grass is to live.

Of course, a screwdriver is one of the most popular tools used today for coin retrieval. Many successful hobbyists swear by them for digging and recovering coins faster, better and with less damage to sod than with any other tool. After pinpointing, they recommend pushing the screwdriver into the ground about two to three inches behind the coin, sticking it in at a 45-degree angle about five inches deep. Of course, you'll want to use a screwdriver with a dull point to keep from scratching your treasure if you should accidentally punch the point into it. Now with your screwdriver inserted five inches deep, you can push forward and to the left, making a slit in the ground three to five inches long. Then make the same slit to the right, with the two slits leaving a "V-shaped" piece of sod which you lift and push forward, swinging it up out of the ground.

After you have retrieved your treasure, the sod will fall back into the hole in the exact place it came out, and the grass roots will not die. This is especially true if you don't cut roots of the grass by making your "V," but merely force most of the roots from the ground. The hobbyists who use screwdrivers are convinced that most park caretakers would much rather see treasure hunters use a screwdriver than a knife!

Here's a slightly different retrieval method for use in parks and other areas where the hobbyist must be careful not to damage the sod. After pinpointing, carefully insert your dull-pointed probe into the ground until you touch the treasure you are seeking. This will inform you of its exact depth. Then insert a heavy duty screwdriver in the hole made by your probe, but stop before it touches the object. (Remember, you already know how deeply buried it is!) Rotate the screwdriver gently until you have a cone-shaped hole about three inches in width across the top. It is then usually an easy matter to remove the item with just a little digging with your fingers or the point of the screwdriver. This method requires some practice and skill, especially when probing, because the treasure must not be scratched. To fill the hole, insert the screwdriver into the ground two or three times around the opening. With just a small pressure toward the hole, the surrounding soil and grass fill it in, leaving absolutely no scar.

Inserting a screwdriver into the ground to measure coin depth is a thing of the past when using Garrett instruments. The electronic circuitry computerized depth measuring technique is extremely accurate.

There are other retrieval methods you can use depending upon the soil condition. In extremely hard and sunbaked soil and in frozen ground, it is necessary to use some type of extremely rugged wide-blade pick to actually hack your way into the ground. In softer dirt, the digging is easier, and one of the methods described above or your own variation of it might prove to be more practical and less damaging to the ground.

Regardless of the type of ground where you plan to hunt, you should study all these methods and work out the one or ones best suited to your needs. Remember, soil conditions can be expected to change with the weather as well as with geography. Be prepared, no matter where you hunt. And always remember to make as small a hole as possible and to fill in your hole after you dig a target. Holes are not only unsightly, but they can be dangerous to people walking in the area. Perhaps it might be you! Before filling a hole, however, be sure to check it again with your detector to make certain you have recovered everything in and around it. It's embarrassing to have someone recover a target in the loose dirt of a hole you originally dug and filled. I know—it's happened to me!

Always remember to carry a pen or pencil and paper with you to make notes of your finds and ideas that come to mind as you hunt for treasure. In metal detecting, like anything else, you learn by doing. As you hunt, you will discover your mistakes, and you will develop your own particular style with new and better ways to find and recover coins.

Good luck with your digging, and always remember to fill those holes!

SOME FINAL TIPS

• My recommendations: hunt in the All Metal (zero discrimination) mode for 10 hours or more with any new (to you) detector and dig up everything you detect. Do not expect to become proficient with any detector until you have hunted diligently with it for at least 100 hours.

• If you haven't started using headphones, now is the time to do so. You'll learn how important they really are. You'll hear sounds you didn't hear before and find objects that you couldn't detect just by listening to a detector's speaker. Masking outside sounds also helps you deflect nosy questions from strangers.

• Learn to listen closely to your detector's signals and pay continual attention to its visual display. Develop the skills to interpret what it is "telling" you through its display and sound indicators. I have seen hobbyists pass over a coin only a few inches deep, yet others use the same detector to detect coins at extreme depths.

A most important factor, therefore, in successful detector operation is an alert operator.

- Always try to guess the identity of every target before you dig. Did you guess correctly? Great! If not, keep on trying. You'll get better and better and you'll gradually find more treasure as you learn to leave trash in the ground.

- Hunting with a top-of-the-line detector will not guarantee success. There is no doubt in my mind that as long as it performs basic functions properly, even a poorly built detector will produce more in the hands of an *experienced* hobbyist than a high quality detector will in the hands of a person who does not understand the instrument or is not willing to learn to use it.

- The amount of success you obtain detecting (as with any hobby) will be in proportion to the amount of time and study that you devote to it. This booklet, the other volumes in Ram Publishing's *Treasure Hunting Library* and the videos available from Garrett are designed to help you develop that metal detector expertise.

- Don't be concerned—certainly in those first 10 hours—about how often you're discovering targets or what you are finding. As you recover various metallic objects, you will find yourself getting better and better with your detector. You will become more at ease in using it, and the quantity of found items will grow at an accelerated rate. All through your learning and training period and afterwards through the years you must develop persistence. Stay with it!

• After you hunt for 100 hours and get more comfortable with your detector, it's time to go back over the same areas you searched before you learned how to use your instrument. You'll be surprised at the quantity of coins and other objects you missed. In fact, each time you come back to these places you'll find more, and deeper, treasure and experience fewer problems using your detector.

• Run-down batteries are by far the single most common source of detector "failure." Be sure to check your batteries before venturing out and always carry spare batteries whenever you are searching.

• If your detector has a volume control, keep it set at a comfortable maximum target signal level. Don't confuse volume with audio (threshold) control. You may want to use a set of headphones with individual earphone volume adjustment so that you can set each one to suit yourself. Set the threshold level at the lowest sound level or "hum" that you can hear.

• Use your common sense. Think your way through perplexing situations. Remember that expertise is gained through research, patience, enthusiasm and the use of common sense.

• Garrett dealers can be a big help, especially in your first days with the hobby. Get to know your dealer and learn from his experiences.

• It's more fun hunting with a buddy! Locate others in the hobby, perhaps through a treasure hunting club. You can learn from each other.

• Study information about old coins and their value, which can be surprisingly high. If your research is thorough, you might find good ones and profit from them.

• A gold coin is the goal of every treasure hunter, whether he or she will admit it or not. The key to finding one is research and hunting where gold coins might have been lost.

- Learn from your computer. Check out the Garrett web site at www.garrett.com regularly for information on new equipment and treasure hunting tips. Chat rooms and treasure forums can also be entertaining and informative.

- Don't expect to find tons of treasure every time you go out! In fact, there may be times when you don't find anything. There are times when I don't. But the hobby's a real joy and the reward of detecting is never knowing what you'll dig up next!

- Success stories are written every day. A lot of treasure is being found and a lot of treasure is waiting to be found where you live. Detectors are not magic wands, but when used correctly they will locate buried and concealed treasure. Use a high quality detector and keep your faith in it. Have patience and as you continue using your instrument your treasure discovery skills will continue to improve day by day.

Success will be yours!

GLOSSARY OF TERMS

Every hobby has its own vocabulary. Treasure hunting is no different. Here are a few terms and definitions to help you understand more about this fascinating hobby.

All-Metal Mode. A metal detector setting that detects all metal objects, no discrimination.

Audio Threshold. The background audio level produced when no target is being detected. It is best to adjust the audio threshold to the lowest audible level, and it is also recommended that the operator use headphones when treasure hunting.

Audio Tone. The pitch or frequency of the sound made by a detector. The tone on Garrett's GTI 2500, 1500 and GTAx 1250 detectors can be adjusted on a treble to bass scale.

Cache. Large deposits of treasure that generally consist of money and valuable objects.

Coin Shooting. Hunting for coins regardless of location or era of coins targeted.

Control Box. Contains the metal detector's main circuitry, controls, speaker, batteries and microprocessor chip.

DD Searchcoil. A special configuration of the transmitter and receiver coils to minimize the effects of ground minerals.

Digital Signal Processor (DSP). A highly advanced computer chip used in Garrett detectors and other sophisticated electronic equipment.

Discrimination. The ability of a metal detector to reject a target, such as a pull tab or foil, and accept a target such as a coin or jewelry, based on its metallic composition.

FastTrack™. Garrett's exclusive technology that analyzes ground mineralization and adjusts to "cancel" its effects in a matter of a split-second.

Frequency. The number of times per second the energy transmitted from a detector's coil changes direction (e.g. 7.0 kHz = 7000 times per second). Higher frequencies are typically used to find targets such as gold nuggets, while lower frequencies are best for general purpose hunting.

Graphic Target Analyzer (GTA)™. Exclusive Garrett technology that visually identifies a target's conductivity or ID and also shows the discrimination pattern.

Graphic Target Imaging (GTI)™. Exclusive Garrett technology that measures and displays a target's true size and depth.

Ground Balance. An adjustment made to "cancel" or ignore ground mineralization; may be done manually or automatically.

Ground Tracking. The ability of a metal detector to continuously measure the ground's mineralization and automatically adjust the detector's ground balance setting for optimum performance.

Liquid Crystal Display (LCD). Graphic display that indicates target information, detector settings, etc.

Microprocessor. Computer chip that performs digital functions that make many features such as Target ID and Discrimination more precise.

Mono Searchcoil. Refers to searchcoils with one ring where both transmitter and receiver antennae are located.

Motion Mode. Refers to the setting where coil motion is needed to detect targets.

Multiple Frequency. Indicates the metal detector simultaneously transmits at more than one frequency. Some detectors on the market transmit at two frequencies or as many as 96 different frequencies. Typically, multiple frequency detectors are specially designed to operate in highly mineralized soil conditions and/or in saltwater with improved detection depth and stability, yet lack the advanced target ID and discrimination capabilities found on single-frequency detectors. *See Single Frequency.*

Notch Discrimination. The ability to electronically create accept and reject "notches" for targets while still providing detection of targets above and below these discrimination settings.

Pinpoint. Feature that allows the operator to determine the precise location of a target in the ground.

Pulse Induction. Used primarily for heavily mineralized environments such as salt water or the gold fields of Australia and is found in many of today's specialty detectors.

Prospecting. Hunting for valuable metals (ores) such as gold and silver.

Relic Hunting. Hunting for targets with historical value, such as battlefield items or family heirlooms.

Salt Elimination. A detector's ability to eliminate interference of salt mineralization, which adversely affects detection depth and target ID capabilities.

ScanTrack™. A unique Garrett feature that automatically adjusts to the operator's scan speed to achieve optimum performance.

Searchcoil. Also called the "coil," the searchcoil is the flat disk swept over the ground to transmit and receives the signal that senses the presence of metal.

Shaft. The adjustable stem that connects the control box and the searchcoil.

Single Frequency. Also known as Continuous Wave, indicates the metal detector utilizes only one transmission frequency for detection. With all of its transmission energy focused at one frequency, a single frequency detector typically offers greater potential depth capabilities, better discrimination and superior target ID under most common soil conditions where the majority of treasure hunting occurs. For this reason, single frequency detectors are the most common detectors available. *See Multiple Frequency.*

Super Sniper Searchcoils. Garrett manufactures 4 1/2-inch searchcoils which are especially effective for hunting in areas with large amounts of metal "junk" or for use near metallic objects such as fences, posts or buildings. These are sold under the Scorcher and Super Sniper model names.

Surface Elimination. A detector's ability to ignore all targets located on or near the ground's surface; useful in heavy trash areas.

Surface Mount PC Board Technology. The latest trend in constructing electronic circuit boards.

Target. Any metallic item sensed by a detector.

Target ID Cursor. A graphic indication of the target's probable identity (e.g. coin, gold, pull tab) based on its electrical properties.

TreasureTalk™. Garrett's exclusive voice function found on the GTI 2500 that audibly announces various settings, adjustments and target information continuously or on demand.

Volume Control. The ability to adjust the loudness of the audible response produced by the detection of a target.

RAM BOOKS ORDER FORM

Please send me the following RAM books:
(Please indicate number of copies desired.)

___ *New Successful Coin Hunting* $9.95

___ *Treasure Hunting for Fun and Profit* $9.95

___ *Treasure Caches Can Be Found* $9.95

___ *Ghost Town Treasures* $9.95

___ *Find Gold with a Metal Detector* $9.95

___ *Buried Treasures You Can Find* $14.95

___ *Gold of the Americas* $9.95

___ *New Modern Metal Detectors* $12.95

___ *Gold Panning is Easy* $9.95

___ *The Competitive Treasure Hunt* $9.95

___ *How to Find Lost Treasure** $3.95

* Free with the purchase of any other RAM book or Garrett product. If you do not wish to purchase anything but would like a free copy of *How to Find Lost Treasure*, mail $2.00 for postage and handling to the address below. U.S. orders only. For international orders, contact international@garrett.com.

Please send payment to:
RAM Publishing Co.
1881 West State Street
Garland, Texas 75042

(Order form continued on back of this page)

MAIL-IN ORDER FORM

Add $2.00 for first book, and $1.00 for each additional book ordered (maximum $3.00) for handling and shipping charges.

Total for books	$_____
8.25% Tax (TX/CA residents)	$_____
Handling Charge	$_____
TOTAL	$_____

Payment Options:

___ Enclosed check or money order

___ I prefer to order through:

___ American Express   ___ MasterCard

___ Visa   ___ Discover

Card Number: _____

Expiration Date of Card: _____

Phone Number: _____

Signature: _____
Required on credit card purchases

Name: _____

Address: _____

_____

City/State/Zip: _____